THE POWER BEYOND PERCEPTION - MODERN INSIGHTS INTO THE KENA UPANISHAD

The Power Beyond Perception - Modern Insights into the Kena Upanishad

DR SURABHI SOLANKI

First Printing, 2025

Contents

Preface 1

Introduction: When Knowing Is Not Enough 4

Chapter 1. The Call of "By Whom?" 7

Chapter 2. Limitations of the Senses 12

Chapter 3. The Fallibility of Intellect 17

Chapter 4. That Which Cannot Be Thought Of 22

Chapter 5. The Witness 27

Chapter 6. Self-Inquiry as Method 32

Chapter 7. Leadership Beyond Ego 37

Chapter 8. Creative Intelligence 42

Chapter 9. Ethics of Awareness 46

Chapter 10. The Teacher Student Archetype 50

Chapter 11. Practice and Embodiment 54

Chapter 12. Living Beyond Perception 59

Conclusion: Becoming Knowledge Itself 63

About the Author 66

Preface

Human civilization has never possessed more information, yet rarely has it been so estranged from genuine understanding. Algorithms anticipate our desires, cognitive systems augment our productivity, and networks connect billions in real time, yet the perennial question posed by the *Kena Upanishad* remains unresolved: *By whom is the mind moved? By whose command does the intellect think?* This ancient inquiry pierces contemporary assumptions about intelligence, selfhood, and perception more sharply than ever.

This book arises from a recognition that modern advancement has outpaced inner clarity. Many feel technically empowered yet existentially disoriented. The pursuit of information has become relentless, though the experience of certainty has grown increasingly fragile. In professional domains, analytical mastery is celebrated, yet wisdom, presence, and ethical intelligence remain uncommon. The *Kena Upanishad* speaks to this imbalance with striking precision. It reminds humanity that awareness is not a by-product of cognition; cognition is an instrument animated by a deeper, subtler intelligence.

The intent here is neither to romanticize antiquity nor to oppose scientific rigor. Rather, this work seeks to demonstrate that the contemplative insights of the Upanishadic seers and the empirical discoveries of neuroscience, psychology, and cognitive science can converge to illuminate a unified truth: the human being is more than the sum of perceptual inputs, neural patterns, or intellectual constructs. The frontier of knowledge now requires not simply faster computing or deeper data sets, but a recalibration of the perceiver.

Readers will find a disciplined exploration of the *Kena Upanishad*, anchored in Advaitic philosophy and cross-referenced with modern research on consciousness, attention, metacognition, and creative cognition. Philosophical exegesis is intertwined with pragmatic reflection to support personal and professional application. The goal is to guide the reader from conceptual admiration to lived insight, because ultimate knowledge, in the Upanishadic tradition, is not something possessed; it is something embodied.

This book is written for leaders, thinkers, educators, creators, health professionals, and seekers who intuit that intelligence without awareness is incomplete. It is for individuals who aspire not only to succeed, but to understand the nature of the one who succeeds. It is offered to those who sense that the crisis of the future will not be technological, but perceptual: a crisis of attention, clarity, and presence.

Readers are encouraged to approach this text not as passive consumers of wisdom but as active participants in inquiry. The Upanishadic method is dialogical, introspective, and self-probing. It does not ask for belief; it asks for observation. It challenges the reader to examine the origin of thought, the witness of sensation, and the silent intelligence behind every act of knowing.

May this work serve as a bridge between ancient revelation and modern urgency. May it cultivate mental stillness in a world addicted to stimulation, clarity within complexity, and a sense of inner sovereignty stronger than any external validation. Most importantly, may it ignite the insight that the greatest power is not in what one perceives, but in the consciousness by which perception occurs.

Knowledge evolves. Awareness endures. The future belongs not to those who merely know, but tc those who understand the knower.

Let us walk that path together.

Surabhi Solanki

Uttarakhand

India

Introduction: When Knowing Is Not Enough

Modern society celebrates knowledge at a scale unimaginable to any previous epoch. Devices recite facts in milliseconds, search engines index the collective memory of humanity, and artificial intelligence now generates patterns, predictions, and insights once considered the exclusive province of scholars. In such a world, knowledge has expanded exponentially, yet wisdom seems increasingly scarce. The result is a paradoxical crisis of abundance: a surplus of information coupled with a deficit of clarity.

The phenomenon of knowledge inflation reflects a structural imbalance. Information multiplies faster than the human capacity to process, integrate, and embody it. Individuals possess access to limitless data but often lack a stable interior orientation. Noise overwhelms signal. Certainty becomes fragile. Opinions proliferate, while understanding deepens only rarely. The intellect, once a luminous instrument of discovery, is often stretched into anxiety, distraction, and exhaustion. Attention, rather than information, has become the scarcest resource.

This condition calls for a precise conceptual distinction. Information refers to organized data; it informs. Knowledge refers to internalized information; it explains. Wisdom refers to the discriminative capacity to apply knowledge skillfully; it illuminates. Presence refers to the silent, conscious awareness from which wisdom arises; it transforms. Information is acquired, knowledge is developed, wisdom is cultivated, and presence is realized. The contemporary world excels at accumulation, yet struggles with cultivation and realization. Knowing more does not guarantee seeing more clearly. Understanding concepts does not ensure perceiving reality as it is.

The *Kena Upanishad* directly addresses this foundational imbalance. It interrogates not what we know, but the knowing itself. It asks the question beneath all questions: *By whom is the mind directed? Through what power does the intellect think? What is the source of perception, cognition, and identity?* Rather than adding more knowledge, the text reveals the limitation of knowledge as a path to ultimate truth. It teaches that the faculty by which we seek answers can never grasp the source from which it arises. The Upanishad does not dismiss intellect; it situates intellect within a deeper field of consciousness. It proposes that liberation is attained not through conceptual mastery, but through recognition of the awareness that precedes and surpasses cognition.

This inquiry has profound implications for contemporary life. For leaders, it reframes intelligence as a blend of strategic clarity and inner equilibrium, rather than sheer cognitive output. For educators, it suggests that effective teaching cultivates not only memory and logic, but presence, curiosity, and discernment. For professionals, it emphasizes that high performance without inner stillness can produce results but rarely produces fulfillment. For seekers, it demonstrates that spirituality is not escape from thought, but liberation from unconscious identification with thought.

The twenty-first century demands a new paradigm of knowing. It requires individuals capable of integrating analytical precision with contemplative depth, technological fluency with ethical grounding, and ambition with humility. In such a paradigm, the Upanishadic insight becomes not historical artifact, but essential guide. The *Kena Upanishad* offers a method of inquiry that remains psychologically, philosophically, and cognitively pertinent: it teaches the art of tracing every perception back to its source, every thought back to the thinker, every identity back to awareness.

The chapters that follow will examine this ancient text through a contemporary lens, weaving philosophical exegesis with insights from cognitive science, attention research, leadership development, and contemplative practice. The objective is not to modernize the Upanishad, but to reveal how its teachings already anticipate modern dilemmas. Readers will be invited into disciplined contemplation, practical application, and experiential understanding. This is not a journey toward accumulating answers; it is a journey toward discovering the nature of the one who questions.

When knowing is not enough, presence becomes indispensable. When intellect reaches its boundary, awareness becomes visible. When the search outward exhausts itself, the inquiry inward begins. The *Kena Upanishad* stands at this threshold. It calls humanity to transcend perception without rejecting the world, to refine intellect without worshipping it, and to discover a dimension of being that no accumulation of knowledge can confer.

In the age of limitless information, the deepest advantage is not knowing more; it is knowing from where knowledge arises.

Chapter 1. The Call of "By Whom?"

The Ancient Question That Outlives Eras

When the sages of the Upanishadic age turned inward, they did not ask superficial questions concerning ritual precision or cosmic mechanics alone. They asked a more profound question, one that reverberates through philosophical traditions and contemporary cognitive science alike: *By whom is the mind directed?* This inquiry, preserved within the *Kena Upanishad*, constitutes one of the earliest and most penetrating examinations of consciousness in human intellectual history. The text does not begin with metaphysical assertions or devotional exhortations. It begins with an inquiry into the very faculty of inquiry. It does not assume knowledge; it subverts the very premise of knowing.

The historical context situates this Upanishad within the spiritual and intellectual milieu of the late Vedic period. Ritualistic orthodoxy was giving way to introspective knowledge traditions. External sacrifice was evolving into inner realization. The seers did not abandon the world; they penetrated its surface and demanded to understand its interior principle. In an era when philosophical thought was emerging globally, the *Kena Upanishad* articulated a question still unanswered by empirical disciplines: what animates cognition itself? What is the substratum beneath experience?

This Upanishad is neither mystical abstraction nor speculative theology. It operates through disciplined inquiry, directing attention toward the invisible engine of perception. Its question is not rhetorical. It is catalytic. The Sanskrit word "*kena*" literally means "by whom." The text thereby provokes an existential pivot from object to origin. Rather than asking *what is known*, it asks *what makes knowing possible*.

The Sacred Interrogation of Cognition

The opening inquiry frames four existential domains: thought, speech, sight, and breath. These represent not merely physiological functions, but the full spectrum of human engagement with reality. Thought signifies cognition and interpretation. Speech signifies expression and communication. Sight signifies perception and sensory interface. Breath signifies life force and vitality. The question therefore encompasses every dimension of embodied experience. It demands recognition that human faculties do not function autonomously. They are powered, guided, and animated by something subtler.

This is not a search for a mechanical "first cause" in the sense of later scholastic philosophy. It is an experiential investigation. The sages did not turn to external authorities, cosmologies, or mythic constructs to answer it. They turned to consciousness itself. In this context, *awareness* is not an object; it is the condition for objectification. It is not something one possesses; it is the essence of being. The Upanishad urges examination of the witness rather than the witnessed, the knower rather than the known.

This inversion dissolves the assumption that human faculties are self-originating. Just as the eye sees objects but cannot see itself without a reflective instrument, the intellect can analyze external phenomena but struggles to comprehend the nature of awareness without contemplative introspection. The inquiry "by whom?" therefore functions as a philosophical scalpel. It cuts through layers of identification, revealing a dimension of self that precedes concept, sensation, and identity construct.

Consciousness as the Ground of Cognition

The Upanishadic seers did not treat consciousness as a product emerging from complexity, nor as a phenomenon contingent on neurobiology. They regarded it as foundational, irreducible, and self-evident. To them, consciousness is not derivative; it is primary. Everything else is derived. This position is not asserted as belief but revealed through direct phenomenological investigation. When all sensory and mental activity subsides, awareness persists. When thought pauses, awareness remains. When perception fluctuates, the field in which perception arises is unchanged.

Consciousness, in this view, is not merely awareness of objects but awareness as such. It is the silent witness to experience, the ground upon which cognition, emotion, memory, and identity operate. The intellect functions within consciousness, not the other way around. This insight reorients metaphysics and psychology alike. Rather than treating consciousness as emergent mind-state, the Upanishad positions it as the substrate from which thought arises and into which thought dissolves.

To recognize consciousness as primary is not to devalue material existence. Instead, it reframes the relationship between the experiential world and the perceiver. Matter is not denied; it is contextualized. Perception is not dismissed; it is understood as mediated. The world remains real at the transactional level, yet the deepest truth resides not in objects but in the faculty that apprehends them. This epistemology elevates introspection to a disciplined method for uncovering foundational reality.

Parallels in Modern Cognitive Science

Although contemporary science does not uniformly adopt a consciousness-first model, significant developments within neuroscience, cognitive science, and philosophy of mind increasingly echo Upanishadic intuition. The "hard problem of consciousness" articulated by modern philosophers highlights the unresolved nature of how subjective experience arises from measurable neural processes. Models of distributed cognition recognize that thought unfolds through complex systems rather than a singular origin point. Metacognition research validates the Upanishadic emphasis on the witness function, identifying awareness of thought as a key element of cognitive sophistication.

Neuroscience demonstrates that perception is not passive reception but active construction. The brain does not simply *see*; it interprets, filters, predicts, and organizes. Vision science has demonstrated that the majority of what one perceives is synthesized internally. Memory studies reveal that recollection is reconstructive rather than archival. Attention research shows that awareness is a selective mechanism, not an undifferentiated field. These insights align subtly with the Upanishadic position: the world as experienced is mediated by consciousness, and the content of consciousness is not identical with the essence of consciousness.

Emergent work in contemplative neuroscience further bridges ancient and modern inquiry. Studies on meditation indicate that training attention reshapes brain patterns and enhances self-regulation, emotional intelligence, and cognitive flexibility. Meta-awareness, long emphasized in meditative traditions, is now studied as a measurable cognitive skill. Although scientific frameworks remain provisional and empirical, they increasingly affirm the transformative power of conscious introspection.

Toward a New Epistemic Paradigm

The *Kena Upanishad* invites readers into an inner scientific method grounded in observation of awareness rather than accumulation of data. It suggests that the most consequential knowledge concerns the knower. Rather than discarding intellect, it refines intellect until it recognizes its boundary and yields to a deeper intelligence. This method offers not merely philosophical clarity but practical advantage, enhancing presence, discernment, and psychological resilience.

In an age defined by cognitive acceleration and informational overload, the Upanishadic question remains vital. Technology can expand access to data, yet it cannot substitute for the silent ground of awareness from which true insight arises. Human flourishing now depends not merely on knowing more, but on knowing *how knowing occurs*. The call of "by whom?" remains a compass for those navigating complexity, uncertainty, and the velocity of modern life.

The inquiry continues into the next chapter, where the limitations of sensory and intellectual perception are examined with precision. The path does not reject perception or cognition; it transcends their tyranny by recognizing their source. The journey begins with the question that refuses to be ignored: *By whom is this experience made possible?*

Chapter 2. Limitations of the Senses

Perception at the Threshold of Reality

Human beings navigate the world through senses that feel immediate, authoritative, and reliable. Vision appears to deliver truth. Hearing offers certainty. Touch, taste, and smell present themselves as direct encounters with reality. This intuitive confidence in sensory experience forms the habitual foundation of daily decision-making. Yet the *Kena Upanishad* cautions that the senses do not reveal reality as it is; they provide a conditioned, partial, and interpretive interface.

The sages understood a principle that modern disciplines corroborate: perception does not equal truth. The senses are instruments, and every instrument has a range, a threshold, and a distortion field. Sensory experience filters existence rather than revealing it fully. What is unseen is not unreal. What is unheard is not non existent. What lies beyond the limits of perception does not cease to be; it merely escapes current capacity.

This recognition does not diminish the value of sensory faculties. It situates them within a larger epistemic architecture. The world apprehended by the senses is not denied. It is contextualized as one layer of knowing. When the Upanishad asks who enables sight, speech, and hearing, it is not questioning the practical relevance of sensory experience. It is questioning its supremacy. It asserts that the senses are conduits, not origins, and that their revelations are contingent, not ultimate.

The Epistemic Boundaries of Sensory Experience

Every sensory modality possesses intrinsic limitations. Vision captures only a narrow band of the electromagnetic spectrum. Hearing registers only a confined range of frequencies. Touch communicates texture, temperature, and pressure, yet cannot perceive the atomic structure beneath. Taste and smell interpret chemical signatures, yet provide only symbolic approximations of material composition. Each faculty extracts a fragment of a larger totality.

Perception is further constrained by context, expectation, and prior learning. The brain filters information based on relevance, habit, and cognitive economy. Humans do not see everything before them; they see what fits internal models. This selectivity, essential for survival, also precludes neutrality. Interpretation precedes clarity. Recognition overrides observation. Assumptions shape reality before conscious awareness intervenes.

Ancient seers intuited these limitations. They observed that the senses reveal a conditioned world, filtered through biological faculties and mental constructs. They therefore directed inquiry beyond perception toward the perceiver. Their approach anticipated a principle that modern epistemology affirms: the instrument conditions the observation. Just as a telescope reveals a different cosmos than the naked eye, the mind reveals a different world than pure awareness.

The Neuroscience of Perception and Illusion

Contemporary neuroscience offers empirical validation of these ancient insights. Sensory perception is not passive absorption. It is active construction. The brain does not receive reality; it generates a model of reality. Visual processing illustrates this vividly. Only a small fraction of retinal signals reach conscious awareness. The brain fills in gaps, corrects distortions, and creates continuity where none exists. Optical illusions demonstrate that perception can be confidently wrong. Despite clear sensory input, the mind interprets patterns in ways that do not correspond to external truth.

Auditory perception similarly illustrates interpretive processing. Phonetic boundaries vary across languages, meaning that what one brain hears as distinct sounds another hears as identical. Taste is shaped by memory. Smell is tied to emotional circuits. Touch can be fooled by proprioceptive illusions, as in experiments where individuals feel sensations in limbs that are not present. These examples reveal a central truth: perception reflects the brain's predictive architecture more than the world's objective structure.

Cognitive science identifies a hierarchy of processing in which the brain continually generates hypotheses about the environment, updates them, and reconciles them with sensory feedback. Predictive coding models align with the Upanishadic premise that outer experience is mediated by inner awareness. The mind does not mirror reality; it approximates it based on internal frameworks. Truth is filtered, constructed, and negotiated.

Hyper Stimulus in the Digital Age

The sensory system evolved to navigate natural environments characterized by moderate stimulus, gradual variation, and direct feedback. The contemporary digital landscape saturates the senses with unprecedented intensity. Screens compete for attention. Notifications punctuate concentration.

Visual and auditory streams arrive in dense succession. Information arrives faster than it can be assimilated. The nervous system, designed for survival in organic ecosystems, is now immersed in a technologically amplified sensory field.

This hyper stimulus overwhelms traditional regulatory mechanisms. The result includes attentional fragmentation, emotional volatility, cognitive fatigue, and perceptual habituation. Sensory saturation narrows the capacity for sustained focus. Stimulation replaces reflection. Reaction eclipses comprehension. Individuals are exposed to content that engages sensory and emotional circuitry without allowing sufficient time for integration or meaning-making.

The Upanishadic teaching gains new urgency in this context. When senses dominate awareness without direction, they can obscure deeper understanding. Constant stimulation does not enrich consciousness; it dilutes it. The world becomes louder, yet inner clarity diminishes. Mastery in the modern age therefore requires not heightened stimulation, but refined discernment and disciplined attention.

Attention as the New Currency

In an environment saturated with sensory input, attention becomes the most valuable cognitive resource. Information holds little meaning without focus. Productivity collapses without concentration. Creativity dissolves without sustained presence. Emotional intelligence requires awareness of internal states. Ethical decision-making requires clarity undisturbed by reactivity. The capacity to direct attention therefore serves as the gateway to agency and wisdom.

Economists describe attention as a scarce commodity. Psychologists characterize attention as a limited and trainable faculty. Philosophers regard attention as an essential precursor to insight. The Upanishads treat attention as the conduit between sensory experience and higher realization. The discipline of attention allows perception without enslavement to stimuli, cognition without attachment to thought, and experience without loss of inner equilibrium.

The modern world rewards those who control their attention rather than those who merely accumulate data. Presence becomes power. Silence becomes a strategic asset. Inner steadiness becomes competitive advantage. The path outlined by the *Kena Upanishad* provides an antidote to cognitive distraction: redirect awareness from objects of perception to the source of perception. Train attention not only to observe the world, but to observe the observer.

Toward Perceptual Freedom

The limitations of the senses do not represent failure. They represent invitation. When sensory perception reaches its boundary, a deeper inquiry begins. The Upanishadic path does not reject perception; it transcends dependence upon it. It cultivates a mode of knowing rooted not in accumulation but in discernment, not in sensory dominance but in conscious presence.

The next chapter explores the limitations of intellect and the necessity of understanding cognition as instrument rather than identity. The journey continues inward, from senses to thought, and from thought to awareness, in pursuit of the truth that precedes perception and illuminates it. The question is not how much one perceives, but how clearly one sees the origin of seeing.

Chapter 3. The Fallibility of Intellect

Intellect as Instrument, Not Sovereign

The intellect is among the most celebrated human faculties. It dissects complexity, constructs systems, discovers patterns, and alters material reality. Civilizations have been built upon its ingenuity. Yet the *Kena Upanishad* cautions against assuming that the intellect is the origin of insight. It asserts that the mind does not illuminate itself. It is an instrument, not the source. The power behind cognition lies beyond cognition, just as light illuminates objects but is not an object itself.

In the Upanishadic perspective, intellect functions like a finely sharpened blade. It can cut through confusion, yet it cannot perceive the hand that wields it. It can analyze the world, yet remains incapable of grasping the consciousness that enables analysis. This limitation does not diminish the intellect; it simply defines its proper role. When intellect claims supremacy, it veils the very awareness that empowers it. When intellect recognizes its boundary, it becomes a bridge to deeper understanding.

This insight is not mystical rhetoric. It reflects a structural truth. Intellect operates within time, space, and conceptual frameworks. It processes information. Awareness precedes these. Insight, creativity, moral clarity, and intuition often arise not through analytic deduction alone, but through silence, stillness, and the dissolution of mental rigidity. The Upanishadic tradition therefore directs seekers to refine intellect until it becomes transparent enough to surrender to a higher mode of knowing.

The Paradox of Analytical Intelligence and Wisdom

Analytical reasoning offers profound utility in the domains of science, governance, commerce, and technology. Yet analytical strength does not guarantee wisdom. History offers numerous examples of brilliant minds lacking ethical grounding, emotional maturity, or discernment. A highly developed intellect can coexist with insecurity, egoic compulsion, or delusion. Sophisticated argumentation can serve truth or rationalize error. The capacity to explain does not ensure the capacity to understand.

Wisdom requires integrative intelligence. It synthesizes intellect, intuition, ethical sensibility, and experiential clarity. It recognizes complexity without becoming entangled in it. It sees beyond immediate gain toward enduring consequence. It discerns not only how to act, but why. Analytical intelligence seeks control. Wisdom cultivates alignment. This distinction lies at the heart of the Upanishadic critique.

Modern society often confuses accumulation with insight and speed with clarity. Analytical intelligence can produce efficiency, but wisdom produces direction. Analytical intelligence can solve problems, but wisdom prevents needless creation of problems. Analytical intelligence excels at strategy; wisdom excels at meaning. Both are necessary. The Upanishadic path integrates them by grounding intellect in the stillness of awareness rather than the turbulence of ego.

Bias, Heuristics, and the Illusion of Certainty

Contemporary cognitive science offers empirical confirmation of the Upanishadic insight that intellect is fallible. Human cognition is shaped not only by logic but by evolutionary shortcuts, emotional impulses, and unconscious patterning. Biases and heuristics enable rapid decision-making but frequently distort judgment. Confirmation bias privileges familiar ideas. Availability bias elevates recent or vivid information. Anchoring bias skews perception based on initial impressions. Overconfidence bias inflates certainty beyond evidence.

These mechanisms reveal a disquieting truth: the intellect often defends conclusions rather than discovers truth. It seeks coherence over accuracy. It favors simplicity over nuance. It protects identity at the expense of objectivity. The illusion of certainty therefore arises not from strength of knowledge but from limitation of perspective. This vulnerability underscores why the Upanishad emphasizes humility in knowing. Intellectual conviction may accompany conceptual clarity, yet clarity about reality requires freedom from cognitive self-deception.

The mind's default setting is not neutrality, but survival. Perception and thought evolved to ensure continuity of life rather than comprehension of truth. Intellectual humility becomes essential for genuine wisdom. Awareness of bias does not eliminate bias, yet it enables reflection rather than blind reaction. The Upanishadic stance is not anti-intellectual; it is anti-egoic. The intellect is honored as a sacred faculty, provided it remains rooted in self-awareness rather than self-glorification.

Ancient and Modern Epistemologies

Ancient Indian epistemology centered on direct experience (*anubhava*), reason (*yukti*), and authoritative transmission from realized teachers (*agama*). These modes were not independent;

they functioned as complementary means of knowing. Direct awareness superseded conceptual frameworks, yet rational inquiry validated and refined intuitive insight. The Upanishadic method was contemplative empiricism: see truth, reason about truth, and embody truth.

Modern scientific epistemology emphasizes empirical verification, falsifiability, and systematic observation. Its rigor has transformed human life. Yet it remains primarily object oriented. It privileges external measurement over internal awareness, third-person observation over first-person perception. Science excels at explaining mechanisms, yet remains incomplete in addressing the nature of consciousness, meaning, and subjective reality. When science acknowledges its boundary, dialogue with contemplative traditions becomes possible. When either claims exclusivity, knowledge becomes fragmented.

The convergence between these epistemologies represents a horizon of future inquiry. Neuroscience explores meditation. Psychology studies attention and compassion. Physics confronts the limits of objective observation. Philosophy of mind struggles with consciousness. Each field approaches a threshold the Upanishads articulated millennia ago: the observer cannot be reduced to the observed. The act of knowing is inseparable from the knower.

Toward Integrated Understanding

The fallibility of intellect is not a weakness to be lamented; it is an invitation to maturity. When intellect recognizes its boundary, it becomes capable of serving wisdom rather than usurping it. The *Kena Upanishad* urges a profound reframing: the highest knowledge is not mastery of concepts but realization of the ground in which concepts arise. Intellect refines language. Awareness reveals truth. The former sharpens the mind; the latter liberates it.

In an era marked by data proliferation, algorithmic decision-making, and technological dominance, this principle becomes increasingly relevant. The future will reward not merely those who think rapidly, but those who think clearly. Not those who accumulate information, but those who discern essence. Not those who assert certainty, but those who cultivate awareness.

The next step in this inquiry brings the reader to the threshold where intellect yields to the recognition of that which cannot be grasped by thought. The journey continues from conceptual understanding to experiential insight, honoring intellect while guiding it toward its rightful place as a luminous instrument in service of consciousness.

Chapter 4. That Which Cannot Be Thought Of

The Unthinkable as the Ground of Being

Human cognition operates through contrast, categorization, and conceptual identification. Thought functions like a sculptor: it carves boundaries, creates distinctions, and fashions meaning through differentiation. Although this process enables knowledge, it simultaneously limits understanding. The *Kena Upanishad* confronts this boundary when it declares that the ultimate reality cannot be grasped by thought, seen by the eye, or spoken by the tongue. The principle in question does not merely lie beyond current knowledge; it lies beyond the very structure of knowing.

This does not imply negation or nihilism. It reveals that consciousness, as the ground of all cognitive activity, remains fundamentally non objectifiable. The mind, which functions through images, concepts, and language, cannot turn itself fully upon the source of its own illumination. Thought can analyze objects, but the knower of thought cannot be objectified without losing essential nature. The Upanishad therefore instructs that the truth being sought is not an idea to be possessed but a reality to be realized.

To acknowledge that there exists that which cannot be thought is not an intellectual weakness; it is the apex of intellectual honesty. When intellect reaches its boundary with clarity rather than confusion, humility emerges, and a higher mode of knowing becomes possible. The Upanishadic wisdom calls the seeker to this moment of cognitive surrender, not as abandonment of reason but as the opening of awareness beyond conceptual closure.

The Advaitic Articulation of Brahman

The Advaita Vedanta tradition names the unobjectifiable ground of existence Brahman: infinite consciousness, without form, without boundary, without second. It is pure being free of attributes, not because it lacks qualities, but because qualities belong to the domain of the measurable and definable. Brahman does not exist *as* something; it is existence itself. It does not know as a mental act; it is self luminous awareness.

Advaita distinguishes two levels of truth. *Vyavaharika satya*, the transactional domain, encompasses empirical experience, personal identity, and ordinary cognition. *Paramarthika satya*, the absolute domain, refers to that which remains when all conditioned experience falls away. The Upanishad insists that Brahman cannot be reduced to a concept, grasped through logic, or contained within language, because language and logic arise within Brahman. The search for truth is therefore not a movement toward an external object but a recognition of the substratum of selfhood.

The declaration *Tat Tvam Asi* (You are That) encapsulates the Upanishadic insight. The seeker does not acquire Brahman; the seeker awakens to identity with Brahman. Realization is not discovery of a new truth, but dissolution of the illusion of separateness. When the mind quiets and conceptual scaffolding collapses, the truth reveals itself as ever present and indivisible.

Knowledge Through Unknowing: Apophatic Traditions

The principle that the highest reality cannot be conceptualized is not unique to the Upanishadic corpus. Many contemplative traditions employ apophatic (via negativa) methodology: understanding by negation rather than affirmation. This approach recognizes that language, by its nature, divides and defines. It therefore points indirectly toward that which transcends definition.

Mystics across cultures have articulated similar insights. Early Christian contemplatives spoke of the "cloud of unknowing," where the mind surrenders to divine presence beyond comprehension. Islamic Sufi masters emphasized annihilation of self (*fana*) to merge with the ineffable divine essence. Taoist sages described the Tao as that which cannot be spoken. Zen Buddhism uses paradox and koan to shatter conceptual fixation, guiding the practitioner to direct awareness beyond thought.

These traditions converge on a universal principle: conceptual knowledge can carry the seeker to the threshold, but only silence unveils the truth. The discipline of negation does not reject knowledge; it refines it until only the pure witness remains. What survives is not ignorance but luminous awareness unmediated by mental constructs.

The Science of Mystical Experience

Contemporary research into contemplative states lends empirical dimension to these classical insights. Neuroscientists studying advanced meditation practitioners, monastic contemplatives, and individuals reporting mystical awareness observe consistent neurological signatures. During experiences described as non dual, self transcendence, or pure consciousness, activity decreases in brain networks associated with self referential processing, narrative identity, and habitual cognition. Simultaneously, integration increases across neural circuits, correlating with a felt sense of unity, clarity, and expansive awareness.

The phenomenology of mystical experience frequently includes dissolution of subject object distinction, profound clarity without conceptual content, timelessness, and a sense of fundamental interconnectedness. Participants often report that such states feel more real than ordinary perception, not less. Although neuroscience cannot yet explain consciousness, it acknowledges that awareness can exist independent of ordinary cognitive structures and that certain contemplative practices reliably cultivate such states.

Psychological studies indicate that mystical insight correlates with long term increases in compassion, creativity, equanimity, and resilience. These outcomes align with the Upanishadic claim that realization is not theoretical but transformative. The *Kena Upanishad* therefore stands not merely as philosophical speculation but as phenomenological map guiding practitioners toward an empirically observable shift in consciousness.

Toward the Threshold of Direct Realization

To approach that which cannot be thought is to cultivate a subtle form of discernment. The practice does not eradicate thought; it places thought in proper prcportion. Thought becomes a tool rather than identity. Silence becomes a medium rather than emptiness. Presence becomes the primary mode of cognition. The Upanishadic seeker learns to abide not in conceptual explanation but in direct awareness of being.

The journey requires disciplined inquiry, ethical grounding, and experiential practice. It demands willingness to relinquish attachment to conceptual mastery, not as retreat but as advance toward a deeper truth. Wisdom dawns when the intellect recognizes that its highest function is to point beyond itself.

The next chapter explores the witness principle, the inner observer whose recognition marks a decisive shift from identification with thought to awareness of thought. The progression moves from questioning the capacities of senses and intellect toward uncovering the silent presence that illumines both. The inquiry continues from the boundary of cognition to the essence that precedes cognition.

Chapter 5. The Witness

The Silent Presence Beneath Experience

Every moment of life unfolds within a field of awareness. Thoughts arise and dissolve, emotions surge and settle, sensations flicker and fade, yet something remains constant throughout this changing panorama: the silent presence that observes it all. The *Kena Upanishad* names this presence indirectly, inviting recognition of the *sakshi*, the witness consciousness that does not participate in the fluctuations of mind but illumines them. This witnessing awareness is not an entity separate from experience; it is the substratum in which all experience occurs.

The witness is neither passive nor detached in a nihilistic sense. It is the stable ground upon which the multiplicity of inner and outer events appear. Unlike thought, it does not fluctuate. Unlike emotion, it does not oscillate. Unlike perception, it does not depend on external objects. It is the unchanging context that makes change perceptible. Without this background of awareness, no mental state could be known, and no perception could be recognized.

The Upanishadic sage does not instruct the seeker to abandon life; the instruction is to see clearly the distinction between awareness and the content of awareness. When this distinction becomes experiential rather than conceptual, a profound shift occurs. One no longer inhabits the turbulence of thought as personal identity but witnesses thought as an arising phenomenon. This shift marks the beginning of inner freedom.

Distinguishing the Self from the Thought Stream

Ordinarily, individuals conflate themselves with the movement of thought. A thought appears, and one assumes, "I am thinking this." An emotion arises, and one concludes, "I am angry," "I am afraid," or "I am elated." This identification with mental content forms the foundation of personal narrative and psychological conditioning. Yet the Upanishadic tradition teaches that thought is an event, not identity. Thoughts occur within awareness, not as awareness.

To observe thought without merging into it reveals that thoughts behave like clouds across a vast sky. The sky is not affected by the clouds, nor does it originate from them. The clouds come and go; the sky remains. In the same manner, awareness remains untouched by the content it illuminates. Recognizing this distinction does not diminish the mind. Rather, it liberates it from unnecessary burden. When the witness is known, mental activity ceases to define selfhood and becomes an instrument for functional engagement.

Practical realization of this principle requires disciplined self-observation. It begins with simple inquiry: "What is aware of this thought? What perceives this sensation? Who knows this feeling?" The inquiry is not intended to produce intellectual answers. It is designed to create space between the observer and the observed. When identification loosens, clarity expands. Emotional reactivity diminishes. Insight becomes spontaneous.

Metacognition and Self Awareness in Contemporary Psychology

Modern cognitive psychology and neuroscience offer striking parallels to the Upanishadic witness doctrine through the study of metacognition: the ability to think about one's own thinking. Metacognition enables individuals to monitor, evaluate, and regulate cognitive processes. It separates the experiencing self from the observing self, fostering self awareness and executive control. Researchers identify metacognition as central to effective learning, emotional regulation, and decision making.

Neuroscientific studies show that when individuals engage in reflective awareness of thoughts and sensations, distinct neural circuits activate, particularly in regions associated with cognitive control and introspection. This aligns with the Upanishadic assertion that conscious observation alters mental dynamics. When the mind knows it is being observed, habitual patterns loosen, and greater choice emerges. The self reflective mind becomes less captive to habitual impulses and more capable of deliberate action.

Contemporary psychotherapy also incorporates aspects of witnessing consciousness. Cognitive behavioral therapy trains individuals to observe thought patterns and reframe them. Acceptance and commitment therapy encourages defusion from thought, viewing thoughts as transient events rather than literal truth. Dialectical behavior therapy trains nonjudgmental awareness of inner states. While secular and clinically oriented, these methodologies reflect the same core principle: awareness of experience transforms experience.

Applied Mindfulness Without Dogma

Mindfulness, when practiced authentically, cultivates the witness state. It involves deliberate attention to present experience without attachment or aversion. However, the contemporary mindfulness movement often emphasizes technique over essence. The Upanishadic vision reminds the practitioner that mindfulness is not merely stress reduction or attention training;

it is a doorway to recognition of the conscious ground that precedes content.

Effective practice need not require ritual, belief, or cultural overlay. It demands presence. Awareness of breath reveals the witness of sensation. Awareness of sound reveals the witness of perception. Awareness of thought reveals the witness beyond thought. This practice can be integrated into any context: a conversation, a professional decision, a moment of conflict, or a pause before responding to emotion. The witness is not reserved for meditation cushions or retreat spaces; it is available at every moment.

To apply witness consciousness in daily life, one cultivates proactive awareness:

- **Observe thoughts without accepting them as final truth.**
- **Notice emotional arousal without immediate reaction.**
- **Sense bodily tension and breathe into it without resistance.**
- **Experience surroundings without internal narration.**

This discipline does not detach one from worldly engagement. It enhances clarity, reduces impulsivity, and strengthens compassion. When the witness is remembered, life is lived from center rather than circumference. One moves from reactivity toward intentional presence.

The Emergence of Inner Stability

Recognition of the witness does not eradicate thought or emotion; it places them in balanced perspective. Fear may arise, yet it is seen. Desire may arise, yet it is known. Achievement may occur, yet it does not obscure awareness. Life continues, yet attachment to experience softens. The individual becomes capable of full engagement without losing inner equilibrium. This marks the beginning of true autonomy.

The Upanishadic sage does not seek to empty the mind permanently, but to prevent the mind from obscuring the self. Witness consciousness represents the threshold between conditioned identity and unconditioned awareness. It does not destroy the personality; it liberates it from compulsive identification. The witness does not eliminate life; it deepens it.

The subsequent chapter explores self inquiry as a systematic method for stabilizing this recognition. The journey transitions from observing the contents of consciousness to questioning the nature of the observer, advancing from witnessing to realization of the ground of being. The path continues inward, toward the source from which all experience arises and to which all experience returns.

Chapter 6. Self-Inquiry as Method

The Pedagogy of Questioning in the Upanishads

The Upanishadic tradition does not present truth as dogma to be accepted; it guides the seeker toward recognition through inquiry. Unlike systems that rely on doctrinal assertion or external authority, this tradition insists that liberation arises only through direct realization. Knowledge transmitted merely as concept remains inert. The Upanishadic teacher therefore offers not answers first, but questions designed to reveal the limitations of habitual knowing and to awaken deeper discernment.

This pedagogical approach is dialogical. The guru does not impose; the seeker does not passively receive. Instead, a methodological cadence unfolds: a question, an internal pause, the collapse of an assumption, and a broader recognition. The inquiry *"By whom is the mind directed?"* catalyzes introspection, redirecting attention away from objects of perception toward the origin of perception. The goal is not obligation to belief, but dissolution of error.

Self inquiry (*atma vichara*) operates like a mirror held before the mind. Thoughts, emotions, and experiences reflect back, revealing their transient nature. The Upanishadic method trains the intellect to examine not only the content it considers, but the one who considers. This reversal lies at the heart of contemplative discovery. Knowledge expands not through accumulation but through refinement of attention and clarity of perception. By asking repeatedly, *"Who is the knower?"*, the seeker cultivates an internal stillness in which awareness becomes evident.

Neti Neti and the Liberation from Identification

The Upanishadic formula *neti neti*, meaning "not this, not this," serves as the cornerstone of self inquiry. It is not merely a negation of experience; it is a disciplined recognition of what one is not. When a thought arises, one observes, "not this." When an emotion surfaces, "not this." When mood, sensation, memory, or social identity appears, the same discernment applies. The process strips away layers of identification until only pure awareness remains.

This practice does not deny the empirical world or personal characteristics. Instead, it distinguishes between the transient and the essential. The body exists, yet it changes. The mind functions, yet it fluctuates. Emotions arise, yet they pass. Identity evolves, yet awareness remains constant. *Neti neti* directs attention toward that continuity, revealing that the self is not confined to form, thought, or narrative.

The purpose of this method is de conditioning, not rejection. The seeker learns to differentiate between utility and identity. Thoughts remain valuable as tools for navigation; they are simply no longer mistaken for self. Emotions become signals rather than definitions. Roles become functions rather than prisons. This approach removes the psychological burden of compulsive self reference and enables a mode of living characterized by greater clarity and resilience.

Integration into Modern Contexts

Self inquiry may appear abstract until examined through practical application. In contemporary life, this method functions not as retreat from reality but as optimization of engagement. Individuals navigate complex environments, rapid information flow, social pressure, and emotional intensity. The capacity to separate awareness from mental reactivity becomes strategic.

The following frameworks bring self inquiry into actionable form:

1. Moment of Pause Protocol

- A thought arises.
- Pause.
- Observe: "This is a thought."
- Ask: "Who notices this thought?"
- Resume action from awareness, not impulse.

This protocol interrupts unconscious reactivity, cultivating presence in decision making.

2. Emotion as Information Practice

- Identify emotion without merging into it.
- Acknowledge, "Fear is arising," not "I am afraid."
- Observe bodily sensation.
- Ask inwardly, "Who experiences this sensation?"

Emotions cease to dominate behavior and instead become data informing intelligent response.

3. Role and Identity Differentiation

- Before engaging a task or conversation, note the role being enacted: leader, parent, professional, partner.
- Ground in awareness before assuming role.

- Recognize: "I am awareness functioning through this role."

This preserves authenticity while improving performance within social constructs.

4. Inquiry at Points of Cognitive Rigidity

- When certainty hardens, question: "What evidence supports this? Who is convinced?"
- Observe automatic identification with belief.
- Allow space for alternative interpretation.

This cultivates intellectual humility and adaptive cognition.

5. Silent Checkpoint Practice

At intervals during the day:

- Withdraw attention inward briefly.
- Notice the observer behind perception.
- Re engage activity with refreshed clarity.

This stabilizes witness consciousness amidst activity.

From Method to Embodiment

Self inquiry begins as discipline, becomes perception, and stabilizes as identity. The practice does not seek intellectual resolution but direct recognition. Over time, the boundary between meditation and action dissolves. Awareness infuses ordinary tasks. Complexity no longer overwhelms. The inner reference point shifts from thought to presence. When misunderstanding arises, it dissipates quickly, because one returns to the witness rather than the story.

The Upanishadic inquiry does not produce detachment from life; it produces freedom in the midst of it. Once identification loosens, creativity emerges, compassion deepens, and decisions arise from clarity rather than conditioning. The wisdom of *neti neti* is ultimately affirmative. By removing what is not self, the true nature of self stands unobscured.

The next chapter turns from individual realization toward its expression in leadership and ethical action. The awakened intellect and liberated attention are not ends in themselves; they inform how one acts in a world that needs clarity grounded in awareness. Knowledge deepens into responsibility. Presence becomes power aligned with purpose.

Chapter 7. Leadership Beyond Ego

Leadership at the Threshold of Identity

Leadership, in its highest expression, transcends authority, status, and strategic competence. It becomes an exercise in clarity, presence, and alignment with principles that elevate collective potential. The *Kena Upanishad* speaks to the interior dimension of leadership when it reveals the distinction between the animating awareness and the faculties through which action occurs. In organizational, societal, and creative spheres, this insight translates into a fundamental discernment: leadership grounded in ego seeks control and validation, while leadership grounded in awareness seeks understanding and service.

Ego is not inherently problematic. The Upanishads do not advocate dissolution of functional individuality. Rather, they distinguish between ego as instrument and ego as identity. When ego functions as a relational interface, it supports purposeful action. When ego becomes conflated with selfhood, it distorts perception, breeds insecurity, and undermines judgment. The inner work of leadership begins with recognizing this boundary and orienting decision making toward deeper intelligence rather than reactive self preservation.

Modern environments demand this maturity. Volatility, ambiguity, and complexity require leaders who can see clearly despite pressure, listen deeply despite urgency, and act decisively without personal attachment. The Upanishadic principle that the intellect is guided by a deeper awareness offers a foundation for conscious leadership grounded in humility, discernment, and inner stability.

Ego as Instrument Versus Ego as Identity

Ego serves essential functions. It organizes identity, mediates social interaction, and anchors commitment to goals. Without a coherent sense of self, purposeful action becomes fragmented. Yet ego becomes obstruction when it seeks validation through superiority, resists feedback, or conflates role with intrinsic worth. The Upanishadic teaching clarifies: the ego is a tool, not the self. It must be employed consciously rather than inhabited unconsciously.

A leader identified wholly with ego tends to defend status quo, suppress dissent, personalize criticism, and prioritize image over substance. Decisions become reactive, fueled by fear of inadequacy or desire for control. In contrast, a leader who understands ego as functional construct engages challenges without internal collapse. Critique becomes information, not threat. Uncertainty becomes inquiry, not paralysis. Success becomes responsibility, not self inflation.

Self inquiry supports this shift. When thoughts of pride, insecurity, or competition arise, the leader recognizes, “Not this.” Action follows clarity rather than compulsion. The result is a leadership presence characterized by steadiness and receptivity. Authority is exercised without domination. Influence arises through authenticity rather than coercion.

Humility as Cognitive Strength

Humility, in spiritual traditions, often signifies surrender to truth. In leadership science, humility has emerged as a measurable trait correlated with high performance. Psychological studies reveal that humble leaders make more accurate decisions, foster innovation, and cultivate psychological safety. The Upanishadic understanding of humility aligns with this empirical insight. Humility is not weakness; it is precision in self assessment. It arises naturally when one recognizes that intellect is instrument, not origin.

Humility allows the leader to:

- **Admit uncertainty and seek counsel.**
- **Prioritize learning over appearing knowledgeable.**
- **Value collective intelligence over personal dominance.**
- **Maintain equanimity in success and failure.**

Humility replaces egoic defensiveness with curiosity. It transforms leadership from assertion to alignment. It does not deny skill or capability. It situates them within a larger field of awareness that remains clear even when circumstances fluctuate. The humble leader is not diminished. The leader is expanded, because perception becomes less clouded by self reference.

Case Studies in Conscious Leadership

While spiritual texts articulate inner principles, modern leadership exemplars reveal practical embodiment. The following cases illustrate qualities aligned with Upanishadic insight: clarity beyond self centeredness, intelligence aligned with purpose, and authority exercised through awareness rather than egoic assertion.

The Visionary Who Listened

A technology founder known for pioneering innovation attributed breakthroughs not merely to technical expertise but to disciplined introspection. He practiced solitude before major decisions, viewing silence as strategic necessity. When confronted with conflicting opinions, he asked not, "What validates me?" but "What illuminates truth?" His willingness to revise assumptions and empower diverse thinkers created an organization defined by exploration rather than hierarchy. His leadership demonstrated that profound impact rests not on egoic certainty, but on receptive intelligence.

The Statesperson Who Owned Mistakes

A public leader navigating national crisis once addressed errors not with deflection, but with transparent acknowledgment. Rather than protecting image, he prioritized integrity. His openness reframed public discourse, shifting focus from blame to learning. His humility cultivated trust across ideological divides. This approach mirrored Upanishadic discernment: when ego yields, clarity emerges, and collective progress becomes possible.

The Healthcare Executive Guided by Purpose

A medical system leader faced a period of rapid transformation. Instead of enforcing compliance through authority, she invited inquiry from every level of the organization, insisting that awareness of patient experience should inform strategy. Her practice included daily contemplative check ins, not as ritual but as discipline to ground action in empathy. Performance metrics improved not through pressure but through shared clarity of intention. Her leadership demonstrated that awareness fuels compassionate efficiency.

These leaders represent varied domains, yet each moved beyond egoic motivation toward a grounded intentionality that elevated collective capacity. Their presence influenced not only outcomes but the quality of participation around them.

The Future of Leadership Is Inner Mastery

As the world accelerates, the capacity to remain anchored in awareness becomes strategic. Technical competence, while essential, cannot substitute for psychological clarity and emotional steadiness. The next era of leadership will reward those who cultivate inner mastery not as retreat from responsibility, but as foundation for responsible action.

The Upanishadic path offers a blueprint: recognize ego as instrument, honor humility as strength, observe inner movement without identification, and act from awareness rather than compulsion. Knowledge grounded in presence becomes wisdom in action. Influence grounded in clarity becomes service rather than dominance.

The next chapter extends these principles to creative intelligence, where inspiration arises not from force but from openness. Leadership beyond ego sets the stage for innovation beyond limitation, demonstrating that true power flows not from asserting the self, but from knowing the self that transcends assertion.

Chapter 8. Creative Intelligence

Beyond Calculation: The Nature of Inspiration

Creativity has long been associated with intellect, yet the most transformative breakthroughs rarely emerge from mere cognitive effort. They arise from a deeper intelligence that surfaces when conceptual frameworks loosen and awareness expands beyond habitual patterns. The *Kena Upanishad* implies this subtle truth when it distinguishes between the faculty that thinks and the consciousness that illumines thought. Creative intelligence resides not only in structured analysis but in the receptive state, where insight flows without force.

Intellectual construction organizes known information. It synthesizes, refines, and arranges. Inspiration, however, reveals what has not yet been conceived. It is not assembled; it appears. It does not conform to linear progression; it manifests in sudden clarity. When inventors speak of breakthroughs, artists speak of vision, and scientists report intuitive leaps, they describe a shift beyond deliberate cognition. The intellect participates in creativity, but it does not originate insight. It prepares, refines, and articulates what awareness delivers.

This distinction has practical significance. When creativity is viewed as mental labor alone, effort becomes strained and innovation constrained. When creativity is recognized as collaboration between disciplined intellect and spacious consciousness, imagination becomes fluid. The Upanishadic insight that thought operates within awareness provides the foundation for understanding this synergy. Creativity is not merely what the mind produces; it is what the mind receives when unobstructed by its own activity.

The Neuroscience of Flow and Insight

Modern research into creative cognition corroborates the ancient intuition. Neuroscientists describe two primary modes relevant to creativity: the deliberate analytic network and the default mode network associated with internal reflection and associative processing. Creative insight arises when these networks communicate in dynamic balance. Excessive control inhibits novelty; unstructured wandering lacks coherence. Creativity demands a unique neural dance: structure without rigidity, openness without chaos.

Flow states, characterized by intense absorption, loss of self consciousness, and effortless action, reveal another dimension of creative intelligence. Studies show that during flow, neural activity shifts from the prefrontal cortex, responsible for self reference and executive control, to broader integrative networks. Decision making accelerates, pattern recognition heightens, and action becomes synchronized with perception. Athletes, musicians, researchers, and entrepreneurs describe flow as entry into a field where creativity does not feel produced, but revealed.

Insight research further demonstrates that profound solutions often emerge during periods of rest, daydreaming, or disengagement, when the mind releases control. Brain imaging indicates that moments before an insight, gamma oscillations surge across integrative regions of the cortex, preceded by a quieting of verbal analytic processing. In effect, the mind steps aside, and awareness illuminates a new pattern. This aligns precisely with the Upanishadic suggestion that the deepest knowing arises when thought becomes still.

Meditation as Catalyst for Innovation

Meditation stabilizes the witness state and refines the capacity to access non conceptual awareness. When practiced consistently, it enhances attentional control, reduces mental noise, and increases sensitivity to subtle patterns of thought and perception. Research indicates that contemplative practices improve divergent thinking, emotional regulation, and cognitive flexibility, all essential for creative functioning. Meditation does not impose ideas; it removes interference, allowing creativity to emerge with clarity.

In creative disciplines, meditation can serve as preparation and integration. Before engaging in intellectual effort, a period of stillness aligns awareness and intention. During creative cycles, brief meditative pauses reset cognitive rhythm and prevent stagnation. After creative work, silence facilitates assimilation and maturation of ideas. The Upanishadic principle that cognition rests upon awareness finds practical expression in this rhythm of alternation between silence and action.

Importantly, meditation for creative intelligence does not require mystical orientation. It requires presence, patience, and willingness to observe thought without attachment. When the mind releases grasping, imagination expands. Insight becomes accessible not as chance anomaly but as cultivated capacity. The artist waits without passivity. The scientist listens without assumption. The innovator perceives possibilities before frameworks formalize them.

From Effort to Effortless Excellence

Creative mastery arises when intellect and awareness harmonize. Effort remains necessary, yet it becomes refined, efficient, and precise. The individual learns to recognize when cognition serves and when stillness leads. Energy once consumed by cognitive tension becomes available for exploration. The ego's demand for control softens, replaced by trust in a deeper intelligence operating through one's faculties.

This evolution parallels the Upanishadic journey from identification with thought to recognition of awareness. Creativity becomes not only a skill, but a state of being. Ideas flow not because of force but because obstruction falls away. The mind becomes a conduit rather than a factory. Purpose and expression align naturally.

The following chapter extends this insight to ethical intelligence, examining how awareness informs moral clarity and responsible action. As creativity without wisdom risks disruption without purpose, wisdom without creativity risks stagnation. The Upanishadic path unites both, revealing that true innovation arises not merely from intellect, but from consciousness attuned to truth, responsive to the world, and free from inner compulsion.

Chapter 9. Ethics of Awareness

The Moral Dimension of Inner Clarity

Ethics, in its mature form, does not arise from external compulsion or mere adherence to rule. It emerges from a refined inner substrate; a consciousness that perceives without distortion and acts without inner contradiction. The *Kena Upanishad* teaches that when awareness is recognized as the ground of cognition, action naturally aligns with truth. Ethical behavior becomes not obligation but consequence. Conduct flows from clarity. Responsibility follows realization.

Inner knowledge is not theoretical understanding, but direct perception of the connection between self and world. When one observes that the same consciousness animates every being, exploitation becomes illogical, and compassion becomes inevitable. Ethics grounded in concepts can be overridden by desire or fear. Ethics grounded in awareness cannot be subverted, because it reflects a deeper recognition: harming another fractures oneself. The Upanishadic sage does not practice virtue as effort; virtue manifests as expression of unclouded seeing.

Modern ethics often emphasizes compliance frameworks, external accountability, and social norms. These are necessary at early developmental stages. Yet mature ethical intelligence transcends regulation. It operates from inner coherence. Accountability arises from conscience rather than enforcement. The principle shifts from "I must act rightly" to "I cannot act otherwise." Awareness anchors action in integrity.

Virtue, Responsibility, and Compassionate Intelligence

Virtue in contemplative traditions is not superficial behavior, nor mere abstention from wrongdoing. It is alignment with the natural intelligence of consciousness. This intelligence sees beyond immediate gratification toward enduring consequence. It perceives interdependence rather than separation. When ego identification diminishes, the field of concern expands. Leadership becomes stewardship, creativity becomes service, and personal gain aligns with collective good.

Responsibility gains depth in this context. It evolves from duty imposed by role to a recognition that one participates in a larger field of existence. The responsible individual acts with awareness of ripple effects. Decisions are weighed not only by efficiency or advantage but by their capacity to uplift or diminish others. This sense of responsibility is neither burden nor sacrifice; it emerges from clarity that personal wellbeing is inseparable from the wellbeing of others.

Compassion, in this frame, is not sentimentality. It is not pity or indulgence. It is intelligence that sees reality as interconnected. Compassionate action becomes precise, courageous, and principled. It recognizes suffering without collapsing into it. It supports growth rather than enabling dependency. It listens deeply, responds skilfully, and remains anchored in truth. Compassion grounded in awareness harmonizes firmness and gentleness, wisdom and warmth.

The Societal Impact of Awakened Cognition

Societies evolve through the consciousness of individuals who shape institutions, norms, and values. When leaders, educators, professionals, and creators operate from ego centered cognition, systems reflect competition, insecurity, and accumulation. When awareness informs decisions, systems transform. Priorities shift toward sustainability, fairness, dignity, and development of human potential. Collective flourishing becomes feasible when individuals perceive themselves as participants in shared reality rather than isolated actors.

Awakened cognition therefore represents not only personal liberation but social intelligence. The impact manifests in multiple dimensions:

- **Governance** grounded in integrity and transparency rather than power play.
- **Economics** oriented toward long term value, not predatory extraction.
- **Education** cultivating awareness, emotional intelligence, and critical thinking alongside knowledge.
- **Healthcare** honoring both biological mechanisms and inner wellbeing.
- **Technology** serving human evolution rather than consuming attention and identity.
- **Culture** celebrating depth, truth, and interconnectedness rather than superficial success.

Such transformation cannot be engineered solely by policy. It requires inner maturity at scale. Ethical evolution begins in consciousness before it stabilizes in structure. Societal reform follows individual insight.

Toward an Enlightened Public Ethos

The Upanishadic vision does not isolate spirituality from social responsibility. It unites inner knowledge with external expression. Awareness without engagement retreats from life; engagement without awareness perpetuates confusion. The future demands integrated identity: contemplative and active, introspective and impactful, wise and effective.

The cultivation of ethical awareness requires disciplined practice:

- **Pausing before action to sense intention.**
- **Examining whether decisions arise from fear, desire, or clarity.**
- **Recognizing that truth serves all, while self interest serves few.**
- **Acting from inner steadiness rather than reactivity.**

When this becomes habitual, life assumes coherence. Work becomes offering rather than transaction. Relationships become arenas of growth rather than arenas of validation. Society evolves through quiet revolutions in perception.

The next chapter shifts focus to the relationship between teacher and learner, illustrating how wisdom is transmitted not through information alone but through presence, example, and shared inquiry. The ethical foundation established here becomes the soil in which genuine transmission grows, ensuring that knowledge deepened through awareness flows outward as beneficial action in the world.

Chapter 10. The Teacher Student Archetype

The Sacred Dialogue of Learning

In the Upanishadic tradition, knowledge is not transferred as information alone; it is awakened within the seeker through presence, inquiry, and resonance. The teacher student relationship does not resemble a transactional exchange. It is a sacred partnership oriented toward inner realization. The student approaches with humility, discernment, and sincerity. The teacher responds not with authority as dominance, but with authority as clarity. Together they enter a dialogical field where truth is revealed rather than imposed.

The ancient learning setting, often under a tree or within a hermitage, reflects a deeper symbolism: the absence of distraction, the simplicity of context, and the primacy of attention. The teacher's role is not to fill the mind but to purify the lens through which the mind sees. The student's role is not obedience but openness to transformation. The Upanishad expresses this ethos through questions that strip assumptions and responses that redirect attention from external certainty to inner discernment.

This pedagogical intimacy rests on trust. The student trusts the teacher's depth of realization; the teacher trusts the student's capacity for awakening. The shared commitment is not to belief, but to truth. In this mutual recognition, knowledge becomes transmission rather than instruction, and learning becomes revelation rather than accumulation.

Mentorship and Transmission in Contemporary Terms

Modern culture often equates teaching with dissemination of content and mentorship with professional guidance. Although valuable, these definitions remain incomplete. Genuine mentorship nurtures clarity of thought, richness of character, and capacity for self direction. The mentor recognizes potential in the student before the student fully recognizes it in themselves. The guidance is subtle yet profound: to help the student see without distortion, act from inner stability, and cultivate intellectual and ethical maturity.

Contemporary transmission does not require monastic environments. It arises in laboratories, creative studios, executive coaching sessions, spiritual communities, and research collaboratories. A mentor embodies lived insight. They teach through precision in speech, coherence in action, and steadiness in presence. They challenge ego gently yet firmly. They draw out latent strengths and illuminate blind spots without judgment.

The student, in turn, assumes responsibility for engagement. The seeker listens actively, questions sincerely, examines experience, and practices inner work with discipline. Mentorship becomes a co created process of refinement. The core principle remains unchanged across eras: transmission is not transfer of power, but activation of potential. The teacher removes obscuration; the student discovers inherent capacity.

Educational Models for Inner Development

Education systems worldwide often prioritize analytical skill, technical competence, and measurable outcomes. These capacities matter, yet they are incomplete without inner development. Awareness, emotional intelligence, ethical grounding, and contemplative capacity represent essential dimensions of human growth. The Upanishadic paradigm demonstrates that education reaches fullness when inner clarity complements outer capability.

Models integrating inner development can adopt several formats:

1. Contemplative Academics

Curricula that combine rigorous study with reflective practice, incorporating silence, inquiry, and observation alongside analysis. Students learn not only content, but how to observe thought, refine attention, and discern underlying assumptions.

2. Experiential Mentorship Frameworks

Programs pairing learners with mentors who prioritize ethical depth and self awareness. Reflective dialogue, personal practice, and feedback loops foster development of judgment and maturity, not just skill.

3. Leadership Education with Inner Inquiry

Executive and professional programs integrating contemplative training, values clarification, cognitive bias awareness, and self inquiry. Leaders learn to anchor decisions in clarity rather than reactivity or ambition alone.

4. Community Learning Ecosystems

Collectives dedicated to shared inquiry, where participants study, meditate, and practice ethical engagement together. The community becomes a crucible for awareness, accountability, and compassionate action.

5. Integrative Pedagogies for Youth

Educational environments that introduce self reflection, emotional regulation, attention training, and ethical reasoning early in life. Students learn to manage inner states, navigate complexity, and build character alongside academic mastery.

These models do not require rejection of conventional education. They enhance it by restoring contemplative depth, recognizing that intellect without awareness remains incomplete. Institutions embracing this synthesis prepare individuals not only to excel, but to understand themselves, relate effectively, and contribute meaningfully.

Transmission as Living Example

Ultimately, teaching grounded in awareness transcends technique. A teacher's value rests not in theoretical knowledge but in embodiment. Students learn presence from one who is present, clarity from one who is clear, humility from one who is humble. In the Upanishadic sense, truth radiates through conduct. The student perceives not a persona, but a state of being.

This transmission does not cultivate dependence. A genuine teacher empowers autonomy. Eventually, the external teacher becomes internalized, not as personality but as voice of discernment. The goal of true teaching is independence of wisdom, not attachment to authority.

The next chapter turns to practice and embodiment, showing how insight transitions from understanding to lived reality. Inner knowledge becomes practical virtue; contemplative clarity becomes integrated presence. The teacher student relationship matures ultimately into the recognition that the teacher resides within, and the path continues through one's own awakened awareness.

Chapter 11. Practice and Embodiment

From Understanding to Being

Insight becomes transformative only when it penetrates behavior, perception, and decision making. Intellectual recognition of awareness as the ground of experience remains incomplete until lived in real time. The *Kena Upanishad* points not toward philosophical speculation alone but toward embodied realization, where truth informs conduct and presence infuses action. Practice is not supplementary to wisdom; it is the means by which wisdom stabilizes. Without disciplined cultivation, clarity remains transient and insight remains conceptual.

Embodiment demands continuity. It calls for integration rather than intermittent inspiration. The seeker gradually transitions from seeking states of awareness to abiding as awareness. This shift unfolds through refined attention, disciplined self observation, and alignment between inner understanding and outward expression. The task is not perfection but sincerity and steadiness. The path moves from knowing toward being, from effortful practice toward natural presence.

The Triad of Meditation, Inquiry, and Contemplative Praxis

Three primary modes consolidate the Upanishadic path into experiential reality: meditation, inquiry, and contemplative praxis. Each addresses a distinct dimension of consciousness and behavior, yet all converge toward the same realization.

Meditation

Meditation quiets mental turbulence, refines attention, and reveals the substratum of awareness beneath thought. It stabilizes the witness and increases capacity to remain centered amidst internal and external movement. The practitioner learns to rest in presence without grasping or resisting experience. Meditation is not escape but training in clarity.

Systematic practice includes:

- **Sitting in stillness with relaxed alertness.**
- **Observing sensations and thoughts without interference.**
- **Returning to awareness when distraction arises.**
- **Cultivating silence as a fertile field rather than a void.**

Over time, the boundary between meditative state and daily life softens. Awareness accompanies activity. Stillness underlies motion.

Self Inquiry

Self inquiry investigates the locus of identity. Through the question "Who is aware?" the practitioner dissolves false identification with mental content. Inquiry does not attempt to produce answers but to expose assumptions and illuminate awareness beyond thought. The movement is subtle and continuous. Inquiry functions like a compass, realigning attention toward the source of perception whenever the mind contracts into narrative.

Contemplative Praxis

Contemplative praxis bridges inner clarity with outer responsibility. It involves acting in the world without losing contact with awareness. Work, relationship, and service become laboratories for presence. Every situation becomes opportunity to practice steadiness, patience, empathy, and discernment. This praxis ensures that spiritual development enhances engagement rather than withdrawing from it.

Together, these practices cultivate depth, integration, and resilience. They ensure that realization is tested and strengthened through lived experience.

Breath and Attention as Gateways

Breath and attention serve as accessible and profound gateways into awareness. Breath is rhythmic, continuous, and ever present. It reflects inner state and influences it simultaneously. The Upanishadic tradition recognizes breath as bridge between body, mind, and consciousness.

Practical breath awareness includes:

- Natural observation of breathing without modification.
- Awareness of the pause between inhalation and exhalation.
- Use of breath to anchor attention in moments of emotional intensity.
- Gentle deepening of breath to induce calm and broaden perception.

Attention, similarly, represents both mechanism and medium of awareness. Where attention goes, identity appears to follow. When attention is externalized compulsively, the self contracts into action and reaction. When attention rests inwardly, the self expands into presence.

Training attention involves:

- Maintaining deliberate focus on a chosen object or activity.
- Returning awareness to the present moment when distracted.
- Observing subtle shifts in attention without self judgment.
- Using micro pauses to re center throughout the day.

Breath and attention are not practices separate from life; they are embedded in every moment. Their disciplined cultivation supports continual return to awareness, even amidst complexity.

Integrating Insight into Daily Behavior

Realization proves itself not in secluded meditation but in ordinary interactions. The measure of awakened cognition appears in patience during conflict, clarity under pressure, humility in success, and compassion in response to others. Integration transforms insight into character, conduct, and contribution.

Key principles for daily embodiment include:

1. Awareness Before Action

Pause briefly before speaking or acting. Sense intention, emotion, and clarity. Choose response rather than react.

2. Presence in Routine

Bring full attention to simple tasks: walking, eating, listening, writing. Elevate the ordinary through undivided awareness.

3. Observation of Emotional Currents

Notice emotional stirrings without immediate identification. Allow space for feeling, then act with discernment.

4. Ethical Alignment

Examine whether actions arise from integrity or impulse. Replace self reference with shared benefit.

5. Consistent Reflection

At day's end, review behavior with honesty and kindness. Observe where awareness held steady and where it slipped. Refinement follows reflection.

These practices are subtle yet powerful. They require perseverance rather than intensity. Progress appears as increasing clarity, emotional maturity, and inner steadiness. Challenges become catalysts for deepening awareness.

Living the Teaching

Embodiment completes the Upanishadic arc. Knowledge becomes wisdom when lived. Awareness becomes transformation when applied. The seeker gradually learns to abide as witness amidst action, to choose clarity over habit, and to act with presence rather than compulsion. Spiritual maturity manifests not in withdrawal but in grounded engagement free from inner turbulence.

The next chapter advances this realization toward living beyond perceptual limitation, exploring the possibility of freedom not as escape from the world but as participation rooted in presence. Insight becomes orientation. Being becomes practice. Awareness becomes life.

Chapter 12. Living Beyond Perception

Liberation from Habitual Psychological Loops

The culmination of the *Kena Upanishad*'s inquiry lies not merely in intellectual recognition of awareness, but in lived freedom from the habitual loops that govern ordinary consciousness. When awareness is mistaken for thought, individuals remain tethered to cycles of fear, comparison, and pursuit of validation. These loops arise from identification with psychological constructs rather than direct perception of reality. Freedom begins when one no longer seeks security in external confirmation or identity reinforcement.

Fear often operates as projection of the unknown. When the self is believed to reside in fluctuating conditions, any uncertainty threatens stability. Awareness reveals fear as movement in consciousness rather than intrinsic truth. Recognition dissolves compulsion. Comparison arises from mistaken perception of separation and insufficiency. When identity shifts from egoic structure to pure awareness, comparison loses momentum. Internal competition yields to quiet confidence. Validation seeking reflects the desire for recognition to confirm self worth. Awareness unmasks this dynamic, revealing that genuine security arises from inner clarity rather than external approval.

Living beyond perception does not require suppression of these tendencies. It requires recognition of their unreal foundations. When awareness becomes primary, psychological loops weaken, and action arises from grounded intention rather than reactive conditioning. This is not withdrawal from human experience, but liberation within it. Individuals who recognize awareness as their essence engage fully while remaining inwardly free.

Conscious Participation in the World

Spiritual realization often invites misunderstanding. Some assume that transcending perception suggests disengagement from worldly life. The Upanishadic vision offers a different resolution: active participation informed by awareness rather than ego. Life becomes a field for expression of clarity, compassion, and discernment. Responsibilities continue, yet the internal posture shifts. One acts without attachment to outcome, responds rather than reacts, and contributes without seeking personal inflation.

Conscious participation means relating to work, relationships, creativity, and leadership with presence. Challenges are met with steadiness rather than anxiety. Success does not inflate identity, and failure does not diminish intrinsic worth. Social interaction becomes opportunity to embody integrity rather than arena for validation. Engagement becomes act of service rather than expression of personal agenda.

This orientation does not reduce ambition. It purifies its motive. Purpose becomes aligned with inner truth rather than external comparison. Vision becomes expansive, yet grounded in humility. Influence arises naturally through clarity of being rather than assertion of dominance. Individuals who live this way do not disappear into meditation; they become anchors of presence within dynamic environments. Their contribution rests not only in achievement, but in quality of consciousness they introduce into collective experience.

Cultivating Stillness in High Performance Contexts

Modern environments demand speed, adaptability, and innovation. Many assume that inner stillness conflicts with high performance. The Upanishadic insight reveals the opposite. Stillness enhances precision, resilience, and creative intelligence. When attention is undistracted and emotion stable, performance improves. Stillness does not slow action; it refines it. It removes noise, sharpens discernment, and enables sustained excellence.

Cultivating stillness in high pressure settings involves intentional practice. Micro pauses during decision making allow clarity to emerge. Deep breathing resets attention during stress. Periodic silence replenishes cognitive resources. Prioritizing presence sustains intuition. Leaders who integrate stillness demonstrate superior crisis navigation. Creators who honor quiet insight generate novel ideas. Professionals anchored in awareness maintain equilibrium under complexity.

Stillness is not idle absence of thought. It is poised alertness. It is the capacity to remain inwardly undisturbed while responding effectively to external demands. Such stillness evolves from consistent practice and sincere inquiry. Over time, it becomes natural posture rather than deliberate technique.

A Life Rooted in Awareness

Living beyond perception means inhabiting the world without internal fragmentation. The senses continue to function, the intellect continues to analyze, and emotions continue to arise, yet awareness remains primary. Identity no longer contracts into transient phenomena. Experience unfolds without possession or resistance. One participates, creates, loves, and strives, yet remains anchored in the silent ground beneath thought.

This state is not reserved for sages secluded from society. It is available to all who cultivate discernment, consistency, and sincerity. The teachings of the *Kena Upanishad* point toward a life where inward clarity illuminates outward engagement. Freedom is lived not as escape from existence, but as harmonious presence within it.

The final realization is simple and profound. Awareness precedes perception. Being precedes identity. When one abides in this recognition, life becomes expression of truth rather than pursuit of it. Stillness and action unify. Clarity guides effort. Consciousness shines through conduct.

The journey that began with the question *"By whom is the mind directed?"* concludes with direct understanding: thought, perception, and identity are instruments of a deeper intelligence. To live beyond perception is to live from that intelligence, participating fully in the world while resting in the timeless ground of awareness.

Conclusion: Becoming Knowledge Itself

Returning to the First Question

The inquiry that animates the *Kena Upanishad* reverberates across centuries: *"By whom is the mind directed?"* This question inaugurates a journey that cannot be completed by intellect alone. It dismantles the assumption that thought is sovereign and redirects attention toward the source of thought. At the outset, this appears as philosophical puzzle; by the end, it stands revealed as existential invitation. The seeker recognizes that the one who questions cannot be observed as an object, for the questioner is the light of awareness itself.

Re-examining the opening inquiry after traversing the path of perception, intellect, witnessing, and embodiment reveals a radical shift. The question is no longer external, posed to a text or tradition. It becomes a living inquiry within one's own consciousness. The search transitions from direction to identity, from epistemology to ontology. The seeker discovers that the faculty seeking knowledge and the essence that *is* knowledge converge in the same luminous awareness. The Upanishadic journey completes not through accumulation of answers, but through dissolution of misidentification.

From Knowing to Being

Modern culture venerates information—measured in data, consumed in fragments, circulated with speed. Yet the *Kena Upanishad* reminds us that true power lies not in possessing knowledge, but in *becoming* knowledge. To know truth intellectually is preliminary; to embody truth as one's very nature is culmination. Knowledge shifts from external acquisition to internal recognition. This is the movement from informational intelligence toward existential clarity.

Being knowledge itself implies living from undivided awareness. It manifests as steadiness in uncertainty, depth in action, and authenticity in relationship. It does not exclude intellect; it elevates it beyond insecurity and struggle. Being knowledge is not passive; it is dynamic presence, capable of discernment, creativity, and compassionate agency in the world. Awareness becomes not refuge from life but foundation for engaged, ethical, and visionary participation.

The transition from knowing to being therefore stands as the essential threshold of maturity. It marks the moment when inquiry ceases to be method alone and becomes mode of living. The distinction between practice and existence softens. Awareness does not visit the mind intermittently; it infuses it. Through this integration, individuals no longer chase certainty, success, or approval. They operate from clarity, sufficiency, and purpose.

A Vision for Conscious Humanity and Future Leadership

Humanity stands at an evolutionary inflection. The accelerating complexity of global systems, the intensification of technological power, and the fragility of collective trust demand new modes of leadership and being. Knowledge alone cannot safeguard the future; only consciousness capable of wielding knowledge wisely can. The Upanishadic vision offers a paradigm suited to this moment: liberation through inner understanding, service guided by presence, and leadership sourced from awareness rather than ego.

Future leadership will not be defined merely by strategic acumen or technical competence, but by clarity of identity, emotional steadiness, and depth of perception. Leaders who embody awareness will build organizations anchored in trust and creativity rather than fear and control. Educators who integrate inner development will cultivate learners who think critically and act ethically. Innovators grounded in consciousness will deploy technology to elevate human potential rather than constrain it. Citizens rooted in awareness will choose cooperation over division, foresight over reaction, and dignity over domination.

A conscious humanity requires individuals who live not as isolated minds but as expressions of shared awareness. This does not erase individuality; it ennobles it. The flowering of collective intelligence emerges through awakened individuals acting with presence, courage, and humility. The Upanishadic path therefore points not backward to ancient contemplation alone, but forward toward a civilization aligned with inner wisdom.

To become knowledge itself is to realize that awareness is not personal property but universal essence. It is to stand in the world with quiet certainty, seeing clearly, acting justly, and loving without fragmentation. The journey continues beyond these pages, not through pursuit of more thought, but through refinement of perception and steadfast embodiment of truth. The question that opened the path remains eternally alive, not as problem to solve, but as compass pointing to the ever present ground of being.

About the Author

Dr. Surabhi Solanki is an author, philosopher, and former physician whose work brings the depth of Advaita Vedanta into the modern search for clarity, consciousness, and inner freedom. With a background in medicine and a lifelong dedication to contemplative inquiry, she writes at the intersection of ancient wisdom and contemporary human development.

Her books reinterpret classical texts such as the Upanishads, the Bhagavad Gita, and Shankaracharya's commentaries, making their timeless insights accessible to today's readers. Her approach blends rigorous thought, experiential understanding, and a commitment to genuine transformation. She guides individuals toward a life of presence, discernment, and purposeful action rooted in awareness.

As a self-published author and educator, she continues to build a body of work that inspires seekers, professionals, and leaders to move beyond information and awaken their highest potential. Her mission is to help readers recognize the ground of consciousness within themselves and live from that clarity with strength, compassion, and authenticity.

Official Website: drsurabhisolanki.com
Email: drsurabhisolanki@gmail.com

9 789356 260344

Printed at Repro India Ltd.